THE PIT

THE PIT

TARA BORIN

2021

NIGHTWOOD EDITIONS
P.O. Box 1779
Gibsons, BC V0N 1V0
Canada
www.nightwoodeditions.com

COVER DESIGN: Angela Yen
COVER ART AND ILLUSTRATIONS: Karen Thomas
TYPESETTING: Shed Simas / Onça Design

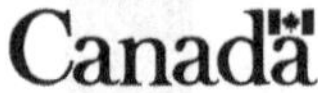

Canada Council for the Arts Conseil des Arts du Canada

Nightwood Editions acknowledges the support of the Canada Council for the Arts, the Government of Canada, and the Province of British Columbia through the BC Arts Council.

This book has been produced on 100% post-consumer recycled, ancient-forest-free paper, processed chlorine-free and printed with vegetable-based dyes.

Printed and bound in Canada.

LIBRARY AND ARCHIVES CANADA CATALOGUING IN PUBLICATION
Title: The pit / Tara Borin.
Names: Borin, Tara, author.
Description: Poems.
Identifiers: Canadiana (print) 2020035227X | Canadiana (ebook) 20200352342 | ISBN 9780889713949 (softcover) | ISBN 9780889713956 (HTML)
Classification: LCC PS8603.O75 P58 2021 | DDC C811/.6—dc23

The Westminster Hotel in Dawson City, Yukon, known locally as the Pit, has been in operation since the early 1900s. The Pit is the Yukon's oldest and longest running bar and hotel, with sloping floors, shared bathrooms upstairs, and some of the most interesting characters you could ever hope to meet. Over the years, it's inspired artwork in many different mediums (including gingerbread) and I hope it will continue to do so for years to come.

This book is for everyone who has found home at the Pit, for better and for worse.

CONTENTS

THE HARD STUFF

LAST CALL

BEER PARLOUR

DESIRE PATHS

In the long absence
of light,
a husky's howls drive us
from our singular

cells to trace paths
pressed in snow:
they bisect the frozen river,
vacant lots,
the barren school field—

all roads lead
to the Pit.

Cold air smokes
as we pull open the door.
Hard to heat a room so big
in weeks of forty below—

we keep our toques on,
learn to flirt in our parkas,
dance in our winter boots.

Held in perpetual
Christmas lights' glow,
curtains drawn against the street,
we pull hands from pockets
to lay bare our secrets
like dark gems.

They glint among small change,
crumpled General Store receipts,
bits of loose tobacco—

we palm them across the bar,
leave them
at the bottle-lined altar
in exchange for an ounce
of forgetting
swirled golden in a glass.

Here is where we find
the shortest distance
to each other:

bar top, schnapps sticky,
plywood dance floor
that feels like it could give
at any moment,
the house band a jukebox
onstage.

Last-call crush,
we open our arms,
make love to the room,
tip the bartender
and stumble into the street,
faces turned up like children
to catch whirling stars
on our tongues.

CHURCH KEY

Found rattling about in the kitchen drawer of a rented house, the handle worn where folded fingers grip, engraved *Maprosa* darkened with tarnish. I take it for my own, take it to my Friday night shift. Bustling up and down the length of the bar I pop the tops off bottles lined up in a row then turn to mix a rye and ginger all with the key tucked neatly in my hand: my secret to speed. Between beers I turn it over and over, the flat of it gently slapping my palm. I am never without it. I wonder what epiphanies it unlocked before me. It opens the door to relief, sanctuary from the daily assault. Sanctuary from lonely social housing apartments. Sanctuary from the past that haunts you, the things you can't control, the things done to you and done to you. I'll guide you through the darkness into the amber light, to a congregation of familiars. My church key always fits, snicks inside whatever lock you're bound by—it will always let you in.

LIST OF DUTIES IN A SUBARCTIC DIVE BAR

If the temperature outside is twenty-five below
        or colder
leave all the faucets running and flush the toilets
        hourly.

R. has a two-drink limit. A. likes a coaster. Remember,
        Mrs. O. takes a chilled pilsner glass
with her bottle of Blue. Never
        keep her waiting.

If someone reveals residential school horrors,
        listen with your whole body.

If a customer becomes unresponsive
        and overdose is suspected,

call the nursing station, then administer the naloxone
        kept behind the bar.
Be sure to write everything down in the incident book.
        This is your therapy.

At the end of each shift, pour a kettle of boiling water
        into the ice well drain. It keeps down the bioslime.

Wrap your cash in the blue vinyl bag and feed it
        to the Snake.

You are entitled to one staff drink. Choose wisely.

SUNDAY MORNING COMING DOWN

The regulars gather
on a Sunday morning,
midsummer sun
as hard as sin
and I minister
to their hangovers
and mine.

Tourists toe the sill,
take pictures without asking,
order pints of Yukon Gold
as if that's what
the locals do.

There's a painting
over the bar
of two men fighting
for a drunk and cheering crowd—
this morning
they spring to life
and tumble
                    out
into the street:
dust-scuffle,
faces red and straining,
each punch
a lost connection.

I'm calling the cops,
I yell from inside,
        (though we know
        they'll never come).

The regulars
shake their heads
while the tourists laugh,
crowd the door and
take more pictures—
Aren't we lucky
to be here today.

FATHER'S DAY

A flight of fathers
tends to their ghosts,
buys beers
with pocket change pooled
between them.

They pull folded photos
from duct-taped wallets or
conjure kids on cracked
phone screens.

Spent shoulders draw back,
rough chins jut out
over sunken chests—

she's on the honour roll
he gets into a lot of trouble
if anyone hurts her
that's my boy

On the desk in the office
upstairs, a framed snapshot
of a curly-haired baby;

their dad counts last night's cash—
pencils, cocaine, calculator
lined up on the desk
beside him.

Our Little Angel of Lost
Opportunity,
a father's reminder to go home,
their chubby hand reaching
for what they cannot touch.

TOTAL ECLIPSE

At the window, they witness
the rusted moon, shadow-eaten

their backs to the near-empty bar
breath coalesced

on cold glass
shoulders a second   apart.

Her spine sings
with syzygy.

He lays his empty bottle
on its side along the windowsill,

doesn't take his eyes
from the sky.

She can't resist a frontman,
the way he fingers

the fretboard
all sweat and swagger,

lips hovering over the mic
as he sneers some Rolling Stones cover.

This one is too old for her.
Has told her that he broke it off

with his daughter's mother and
she believes him.

When the bar thrums thick with people
thirsty for her attention,

she serves him first:
as she bends

to place the beer
next to him onstage

she doesn't break
his gaze.

Outside, shadows disgorge
the unattended moon.

CRIBBAGE & CHILL

We set up the crib board
between us,
your thigh next to mine
at the bar.
I win the cut with a six
to your nine, shuffle
and deal from the bottom,
my fingers flick
a half dozen cards each,
you slip a pair into my crib
then cut the deck,
a johnny for two—
I get a head start.
We're on a run,
pegging off each other:
fifteen-two
twenty for two
twenty-five for six
thirty-one for two.
You count your cards
slow,
keep me waiting—

a triple run

and my hand's worth nineteen.

You pull away—

I'm stuck chasing

behind.

Skunk me, baby,

I'd lose to you

any time.

ROOMS FOR RENT

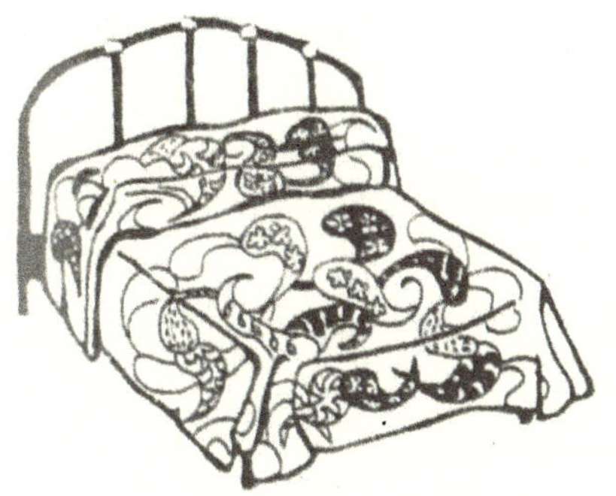

HEARTBREAK HOTEL

She smokes a cigarette in her underwear by the tiny square of window, watches ravens tear into a dumpster in the puddled back alley. Eleven p.m. sunset smoulders into summer. In her room, empty takeout containers bloom across the bare wood floor, chow mein and ginger beef spice the air. Bedspread wilts from a tired bed; her life tumbles from the same duffle bag she arrived with a year ago. Love born in dust and black spruce. Drinking the expensive wine in the willows, the bottle passed between them as though it had cost much less. Slick thighs. When the cranes flew south, they took their love between four walls: a drafty cabin, bed in the corner. Lips traced in kerosene glow. They fed each other tinned mussels, cream crackers, licked oil from fingers. With each snowfall, the cabin seemed to shrink. As winter unravelled into spring, she watched her lover pace the walls, wild. The wood stove continued to eat whole swaths of forest in exchange for a heat that was too much to bear or else not enough. They broke like the river when the gulls returned. Now she's alone in a cheap hotel room with the muck of all things done that cannot be undone. She can hear life going on, the rise and fall of it, classic rock and bar-top banter. She ashes into an empty beer can. How many heartbreaks has this room held?

HOME

You leave your shampoo
in the shared bathroom,

take your morning coffee
each day in the bar downstairs,
CBC news on mute,
telling the bartender your dreams,

your sleep schedule formed
around opening hours,
your lullaby last call
slurring into the streets below.

Friends ascend the narrow
staircase to your room,
bring six-packs of Kokanee
and a bag of weed, just for a visit.

You buy the last straggly cyclamen
at the General Store and place it
on the windowsill,

chop an onion on the beat-up
antique dresser,
add it to the slow cooker
you found at the Free Store
out at the dump.

No longer just
a cheap flop
for a few days—

you could have a dog here,
like the guy down the hall.

WRAITH

Black fur hat and dark
sunglasses
she wanders the hotel's
            nicotine halls
            carpet worn to a shine
rattles the doorknobs
in the hours before
your hangover.

Outside the bathroom
she grips your arm,
whispers,

I can't find
my room.

My husband
will kill me.

She presses a key
into your palm,
faded numbers on the tag—
you lead her
down sloping halls
to the corresponding door

left open a crack—
you push it open,

television blares
static noise
into an empty room.

You blink
in the bare bulb's
rude glare,

then turn to find yourself
alone—

she's left you
holding the key.

DRUNK TANK

Too many rye sodas and
someone joking that
your failed marriage was
his mid-life crisis

turned the evening
maudlin
and has ricocheted you
here, to this room that

won't
stop
spinning.

You lie tangled in a fugue,
listening to the bar closing
below you:
music cuts out,
murmur of conversation
moves into the distant street.

Footsteps heavy on the stairs,
in the hallways,
long after you think
you've gone to sleep—

you'll die here, surely.

The doorknob turns
slowly to the left.
To the right.
Is still—

ghosts of blackouts past,
seeking solace.
You welcome them inside,
spoon together
on the sagging bed.

LAST NIGHT

A pair of
burlesque dancers
in the third-floor washroom
glitter and preen
before the bare mirror

down the hall

people clown-car
into the honeymoon suite,
pass around joints,
await the clandestine show—
tattoo artist fires
a T-shirt cannon
into the crowd lined up

below

the bouncer scans the packed bar shakes hands with the band as they arrive for the gig lead singer in a black pleather fishnet bodysuit elbows through the crowd grabs a beer bottle by the neck and drains it drunk patrons sprawl in strangers' laps whisper wet in their ears rush the bar rush the stage three to a bathroom stall doing lines off the back of the toilet ACAB scrawled on the wall

we're all so close we could lick the sweat off upper lips taste tequila
burnt breath

and the lineup

trails out

into

the

snow.

Come talk to me,
I'm that girl—
you are beautiful and
every thought you have
is a real thing,
transient and shifting,
like water.

Listen:
pride is a riot and
relationships suck.
You should dump him
before he dumps you,
dingus.

THE REGULARS

DEAREST

His fingers quake
as he counts his change—
falls short,

tries to quiet them
around his coffee cup.
I spot him two fifty
for a pint,

he drinks deep;
soon, his fingers
will settle.

He plays crib for money
he doesn't have;
used to play for smokes
in jail,
so he learned to peg
real quick.

He wins another pint
and his face brightens
like the sun over the hills
in mid-January.

He sings along to the radio,
his tenor full
of gravel—
pulls me in,
my off-
key warble,

winks at me and I wonder
who he'd be
in a kinder timeline.

I long to comb my fingers
through his unwashed
hair, salt & pepper,
smooth Blistex
over his chapped lips—
I've never been any good
at keeping
the worn mahogany counter
between us.

Sometimes I see him,
a little boy,
legs dangling from the stool,
kicking muddy boots
against the bar.

I want to take him
home, feed him
anything other
than whisky and beer

but for now
that's the only medicine
we know.

NIGHT JANITOR

Hears God
in the electricity,
keeps
religious pamphlets
in the pockets
of his insulated coveralls.

When the waters rise
in the basement
he whispers a prayer, then
hides the mops.

Each night he sifts
through the contents
of the dustbin:

condom wrapper
beer caps
damp mitten
plastic straws
cigarette butts
empty chip bags
earring

catalogues each sin,
slips it
into a hole
in the drywall.

OFFERING

She fidgets
at a table across the room
in a slant of afternoon light
          my lone customer
sipping

a glass of Canadian
with a splash
of Clamato.

She jumps up,
glides over to where
I dust the dead
crowding the wall.

Her drugstore reading glasses
tangle with a pair of sunglasses
pushed back over her faded hair,
watery blue eyes wide—

she confides she's got a new job
housekeeping
at the Downtown,

says she'll pay me back
the twenty she owes me
real soon.

Her arm sweeps across
the empty room and
she offers me a glimpse
of her past:

she had the skating rink
all to herself

the attendant
put on music and she
circled the rink—
push
and glide.

As she tells me the story
she closes her eyes,
her arms float up
to shoulder level,

chapped fingers full
of sudden grace.

She sways
in a remembrance
of motion

and I see her
made new.

PORTRAIT OF THE WATER-WITCHER

Bear-faced,
he'll tow you
out of the ditch

drop a cord of fire-kill
in your yard
once the snow flies.

Half a cuppa coffee
in the mornings,

whisky at happy hour,
he holds up the far end
of the bar.

In late summer,
smokes fish,
brings it

in a greasy paper bag
to share on a Friday night,
salt on your tongue.

Town water-witcher,
two thin L-shaped wires held loose
in his soot-blackened hands,

he paces the land,
silent but for the faint whistle
of his breath.

When cryptesthesia
pulls the wires positive
he'll pronounce,

There—
your water's there.

PORTRAIT OF THE RETIRED BARMAID

Canucks game turned up
on the clock radio,

rye and Coke in a Mason jar
next to the Pond's Cold Cream,

she leans closer to the bathroom mirror
to line her thin lips coral,

hooks a pair of sterling butterflies—
crystal accents flashing—
into her soft earlobes,

knots a red silk scarf at her throat.

She leans back, takes a drag
from the cigarette

seething smoke
in the ashtray by the sink

and pats her greying salon-set curls.
Snaps off the radio, her team

about to lose,
blows kisses to her cockatiel,
crest bobbing in his cage,

to the photos of her grandbabies
crowding the walls.

She slips into her old bomber jacket
with the bar's faded pink logo
on the back.

One last look in the mirror:
Still got it, Sugar,

best damn barmaid
this town'll ever see.

REASONS

We drink because the sun never sets or
        because it never rises.
To find love, distorted by the empty bottle's lens.
To hush the heart.
To soothe unwritten stories.
We drink the wounds of our parents
                                and of their parents
                                                and theirs.
We drink to dull the throb of an abscessed tooth.
To stop our hands from shaking.
Because it's happy hour.
We drink without even having to think about it,
        because it feels good
                                to lose control,
                                                feels like regaining it.
We drink to see the sky shift above us and
        feel the earth wheel beneath our feet.
We drink our youth until it's dry and then
        we drink to all the ends.
Our wins and losses—
        they taste the same.
To you who would judge us, and you who would join us
        and you who have already gone.

THE HARD STUFF

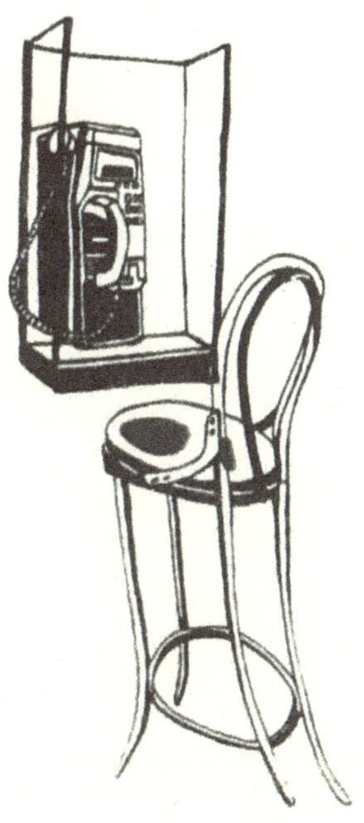

THE ADDICT'S WIFE

It's always cold on his side of the bed.
A tired refrain haunts my sleep—
this time I'm sure he's dead.

In dreams I'm already widowed,
see him wrapped in a sheet
on his cold acre of bed,

last words a debt,
his beloved body rotting meat.
This time I know he's dead.

Awake and left on read
for hours, my eyes bleed.
It's always cold on his side of the bed.

From the beginning, he said
he kept his secrets buried deep.
This time I'm sure he's dead.

Heartstrings worn to threads,
he was never meant to keep.
It's cold on his side of the bed
and this time, I'm sure he's dead.

PUNCH

At the clinic today
the doctor thumbed
a rough patch of skin
on my knee,

wondered if it could be
psoriasis.

She unwrapped
a sterile skin punch:
flash of surgical steel,
bright twitch of pain
under pitiless fluorescent lights—

she took a core sample
of me, in a serious voice
asked,

Do you spend a lot of time
on your knees?

Don't laugh.

See me on my knees
playing with the baby,

cleaning up empty bottles
from under the couch,

pulling weeds
in the garden,

feeding sticks of kindling
to the dying fire,

gathering bits
of shattered glass
in the kitchen—

see me on my knees
beside you
on the living room floor
where you've fallen down
drunk

again.

TELEPHONE

I am the one
serving him beer
after beer, trying not to think
about who is left at home.
It's none of my business, I'm not
here to judge.
I take the rent money, the diaper fund
and break the change down for tips.
When the phone rings, the voice
in my ear is stretched thin
by sleepless nights
and distance.
I pass the phone over,
busy myself cutting limes—
acid stings the cracked skin
between my fingers.
The proud bull's head
watches from the wall
as someone buys another round.

I am the one
cupping the receiver of a pay phone
in a truck stop parking lot
(because we're too rural
for a phone)
baby wails in the car seat
as the first snow blurs the windshield
cools my flushed cheeks

I whisper down the line
is he there
Poke's been hit
by a truck
please
come home
barroom foams
through the receiver
your voice
drowning
in theirs
hang up the phone
settle the baby
drag the dog
off the road
myself
and bury the body
beneath the birch trees
you love so much

ENOUGH

I stand as sober as my axe
in the midst of the bar's
amber buzz—

swing

          the axe,

explode

his beer glass
and crack
the old Formi-
ca table where he sits.

Honky-tonk jangles

silent.

I don't need
a man
to help me eat
the roast
in the oven or
drink the half-sack
of beer
in the fridge or
chop the goddamn

firewood but
        it'd be nice.

At sixteen I carried
a moose calf out of the bush,
its throat ripped out
by dogs—
it was bleating
& bleeding,
its mother
        nowhere.
By the time I got back
to the truck,
my shirt was stiff
with blood.

He called me
Patron Saint of Lost Causes,
has worn me like a medal
next to his skin
ever since.

How many times
have I carried
him out
these years?

How many more times?

AT THE COP SHOP

Getting fingerprinted
for a new job,
my four-year-old in tow.

The handsome young constable
    all angle-jawed, blue-eyed,
    brassy blond highlights
    in his cropped dark hair
leads us
into the depths
of the station,
to a windowless
cinder-block room
where we stand shoulder
to shoulder,
the ink pad
on a table in front of us,
my kid crowding the edge
to watch.

Let me do the work,
he commands,
so I let my hand
go limp
in his—
tendons pop
along its back
a soft haze of hair

creeps from the cuff
of his shirt.

He starts with my thumb,
presses and rolls it firmly,
first in ink, then
on paper.

Repeat for each finger
of each hand.
When he reaches
my ring finger
I am briefly grateful
that the fish-belly mark
left
by my wedding band
has finally
faded
away.

PIT KID

As a baby they played with pool balls
at the staff parties,

were given shot glasses of water
and passed around for photos.

Up for days,
Dad likes to slur on

about his perfect child
to anyone who'll listen.

Drunks call the house
at night, looking for a loan,

and Pit Kid learns their mom's
furious whisper in the dark.

When they're ten,
they play *Super Mario*

with their friends
in the tobacco'd office upstairs.

They're sent down
on occasion for supplies,

stand in the doorway
to the tavern

while their dad
fills an empty beer box

with cans of pop and
small bags of Lay's potato chips.

Their mom, her makeup done,
their friends' parents

crowd around a table
with pitchers of beer,

sing "Wagon Wheel" as someone
abuses an acoustic guitar.

By the time they're twelve,
they switch to soft ciders,

start stealing smokes
from packs left unattended.

Mom talks about taking them to stay
at her sister's place in Ontario.

Dad sleeps on the chintz sofa
whenever he comes home.

He gets sober,
takes them fishing for grayling,

gets drunk,
falls down the stairs.

They learn that nothing lasts.

He wants them to take over
someday, believes it to be a gift,

but they know better.

They dream
of lighting a match,

and not even staying
to watch it burn.

LAST CALL

REST STOP IN PELLY CROSSING

Black leather fringe
swings in my open car window:
a woman I know from the bar
back in Dawson

wonders if I'm going
to Whitehorse,
asks me to do a liquor run,
says she'll get cash
and slides into the passenger seat
before I can say no.

Let's go for a ride,
I'll show you
where I live.

Home of the Selkirk:
dirt side streets, neat houses,
school and playground—
a village beyond
the gas station
not concealed but
never noticed
in my countless trips along
the Klondike Highway.

Her home
a little red cabin,
door chained and padlocked,
a faded sign in the window:
Sorry, We're Closed.

Remember the sign,
she says.
I'll wait for you
here.

I write her name in the dust
on my dashboard
so I won't forget
her request.
Two days later
on my way back through
the sign is flipped:
Come In. We're Open.

She is asleep on the couch
under the window.
I tap on the glass—
she swims up
and out of sleep.

She stashes the bottles
of vodka then offers
to show me around her yard:

delicate bluebells
beginning to bloom
amid the tall wild grasses
beaten down into a path
to the old shack where
her family smokes meat
and fish.

I can't stay, I tell her,
as if she asked.

FLOOD

Customers bring me
bits of rumour like flotsam,
even as the water
surges in—
    ice's jammed downstream
    and the dike ain't gonna hold.

Grayling silver
between tables
that shift

and bob. The regulars
order Budweisers, shots
of Fireball, shuffle their feet
in the silted river

come indoors.
The old tube TV
mounted to the wall
flickers soft
with the Canucks game.

Downed trees rush
along the drowned street,
knock at the front

of the building. Cards are dealt,
an RCMP cruiser swirls by
in the eddy as someone scores
a twenty-one hand in crib, onlookers

mildly impressed.
Neighbouring buildings lift
from their cribbing and jostle
against each other
like drunks commiserating
in the street. Everything

afloat. The Elders
at the back table
agree in hushed Hän
they've seen all this

before. They wade over
to the birchbark canoe
suspended
from the ceiling
over the bar, gentle it

down and paddle away
through the open front door.

ONE FOR THE DITCH

Doc Parsons and the boys
bring him in,

washed and dressed
in his best pair of jeans,

his favourite flannel shirt
buttoned and tucked.

They hoist him on to the bar top,
order a small glass of beer

to place on the lid
of the pine box they made

in someone's garage,
where whisky loosened their tears.

Pints are passed over the box,
careful not to spill.

Women bring in steaming dishes
of moose stew and bannock

while the piano hammers a heartbeat
in the corner.

The tavern fills with parkas
and the warmth of so many bodies

remembering what it is
to be alive.

After, they gather
at the cemetery on the hill

stamp their feet to keep warm
as he is lowered to rest
in the frozen ground.

In the empty bar,
the bartender

thumbs his phone,
picks at the leftovers.

ROMANCE CAPITAL

Ravens circle
a red pickup truck,

lift the edge
of the blue tarp

that covers a stiffening
carcass—

moose antlers spread
        like hands in supplication
full of mineral sky.

In the bar, a man
sets down his beer,

wipes his mouth with the back
of his hand and lifts his voice

to tell the gathered
how he called that bull

right off the mountain,
how it took

three shots
through the neck

to drop him.
Hands cup

his mouth,
shoulders hunch forward—

he utters a low,
urging sound

it brims
with moose-cow lust

and then another
and another

sets down their beer
to offer up their voices until

the whole bar groans
in a chorus of rut.

Outside, the blue tarp
shudders.

Palmate antlers lift:
sky spills over.

Ravens scatter.
Talons clatter on roof tin

as Moose clambers over the side
into the dirt street:

his throat drips gore
like a boutonniere

like a bow tie
and he has to turn his head

sideways and duck
to enter the bar,

a nervous suitor ready
for the promised mate.

THE WALL

When you die,
          if you will it,
someone will print your photo,
slip it into a dollar-store frame
and bring it to the bar.
We'll drive a nail into the pressed tin
of the south wall near the TV
and place you among the others.

You'll gather our dust
in the buttery late-morning sun,
in the hush and glow of winter,

and every so often,
we'll raise a glass,
speak your name,
share your story
so you'll not
be forgotten
in time.

NOTES & ACKNOWLEDGEMENTS

"We'll Never Have Enough of This" is a found poem using graffiti in the women's washroom of the lounge.

"Father's Day" was previously published in *Prism international*, 58.4, Summer 2020.

"Flood" was previously published in *The LaHave Review*, Summer 2020.

"Enough" and "Romance Capital" were previously published in *Prairie Fire*, 40.2, Summer 2019.

"Romance Capital" was adapted for the stage by Friends of the Palace Grand for their play *Cabin of Curiosities*.

My thanks to the Tr'ondëk Hwëch'in for generously welcoming settlers like me to live, work and write on your homelands, and to the land for always holding me through difficult times. Mahsi cho.

This book wouldn't exist without the Westminster Hotel. I owe so much to all of the people who've shared a glass and a story with me at the bar; and to the crew who've been in the weeds with me, pumping out drinks or breaking up fights or just generally bearing witness to some unbelievable and beautiful shit. I'm also very grateful for my studio space on the third floor, where I wrote most of these poems.

To my poetry cohort at the Writer's Studio—Ashley, Bre, Cecil, df, Jane, Janna and Ping, and my mentor Kayla Czaga—thank you. I learned so much from writing alongside you, from reading your work and receiving your comments on my own.

To the writers further along the path who mentored and encouraged me, many of whom I met through the Berton House Writer's Retreat: Anakana, Miranda, Elizabeth, Trish, Sarah, elaine, Dina, Adèle and Sean, thank you for your generosity of time, attention and friendship.

Thanks to Chelene Knight, who helped me get this collection ready to submit.

To Silas, Emma and the rest of the amazing team at Nightwood, thank you for giving this book a home.

Thanks to Jo, who read the very first poem I wrote for this collection and told me: yes, I think you've got something here!

And thanks, as ever, to my parents, for always believing that I could do it.

ABOUT THE AUTHOR

Tara Borin is a graduate of the Writer's Studio Online with Simon Fraser University. Their poems have appeared in *Resistance* (University of Regina Press), *PRISM International, Prairie Fire, emerge 19* and *Best New Poets in Canada 2018* (Quattro Books). They are a queer, non-binary writer living in traditional Tr'ondëk Hwëch'in territory, Dawson City, Yukon.

PHOTO BY ROBIN SHARP